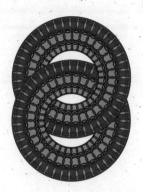

momentum

Catherine Doty

4/8/05

momentum
Catherine Doty

Patrick!
In joy and
friendship —
and with
gratitude for
your
fine
work.

CavanKerry ◆ Press LTD.

love,
Cat

Library of Congress Cataloging-in-Publication Data

Doty, Catherine.
Momentum / Catherine Doty.
p. cm.
ISBN 0-9723045-0-9
I. Title.
PS3604.O684M66 2004
811'.6--dc21
2003046049

Cover Photograph: *Family Snap* © 2004 by Doty Family
Author Photograph by Jody Merritt
Cover and book design by Peter Cusack

First Edition
Printed in the United States of America

CavanKerry Press Ltd.
Fort Lee, New Jersey
www.cavankerrypress.org

Acknowledgments

Thanks especially to Renée Ashley. Much gratitude to Tony Hoagland, Jim Richardson, and Baron Wormser. Warmest thanks to Del Earisman, Jim Lovell, Madeline Tiger, Lisa Rhoades, Ken Hart, Penny Harter and Bill Higginson. Many thanks to David Keller, Bob Carnevale and Joe Weil, and to Robin Locke Monda, Bob Monda, Ellen Wright and Tamara Coombs. Thanks so much, Mel Kershaw and Cynthia Webb. Sincere thanks to the New Jersey State Council on the Arts, the New York Foundation for the Arts, and the Council on the Arts and Humanities for Staten Island, for grants that helped with the completion of this book. Thank you and thank you to my teachers and my students.

A number of these poems, or versions of them, originally appeared in the following publications whose editors I thank for permission to reprint:

Footwork, A Woman Who Liked Babies, Why I Don't Drive a New Car
Grolier Poetry Prize Annual, Momentum, Gratitude
Heliotrope, 3 A.M., Care
Journal of New Jersey Poets, "For May Is the Month of Our Mother," Yes
Louisiana Literature, French Coke
Margie, Mrs. Vooren's Calendar, Outside the Mainway Market
Mudfish, Lassie Comes Home
National Poetry Competition Anthology, Chester H. Jones Foundation, The Hungry Child
Negative Capability, Landscape with Pony Track, Living Room
New Press Quarterly Review, Sunburn
Selections, University and College Poetry Prizes, Academy of American Poets, Home for a While
Written with a Spoon, Figs

NEW JERSEY STATE COUNCIL ON THE ARTS

NATIONAL ENDOWMENT FOR THE ARTS

CavanKerry Press is grateful to the National Endowment for the Arts and the New Jersey State Council on the Arts for its support of this book.

We master the bowl of this temporality by brimming it.
— Li-Young Lee

for Fred, Henry and Willy

for my family

Contents

Foreword

How is it that the daily tedium we begin to experience as children and that swells into the full sails of beleaguered, knowing adulthood is so jam-packed with desolate thrills? How to square the bleary mundane with the unadulterated "Yes" (to quote the title of the opening poem of this collection) that (to quote further) is "blood/banging in the body"? Poems, of course, aren't answers to the great and less-than-great riddles but they may be enticing and bracing clues. Catherine Doty has assembled a whole, marvelous book of such poems whose eyes are warily wide open and whose ears catch every little screech.

Her subject matter is largely domestic: the shards of childhood, growing up, viewing one's parents from various sobering yet moving perspectives, parenting one's own children and the taut mirror that throws back. The scenes accordingly are houses, neighborhoods, yards, the interiors of cars, stores. What is remarkable is how truly she is able to locate the emotional throb that vibrates through each setting, each memory, each encounter. She has a genius for detail in the strict sense of the word. She divines the "prevailing spirit" in each scrap of place and summons it up in details that are stinging yet delicate—"a pill cup/of macaroni"—as she notes in a poem about a mother who upon entering the paid work force is almost dizzy with gratitude.

The stories the poems relate do not open onto grand, declamatory views. They are all the richer for their fidelity to the whole of a particular experience. In this sense, Doty has an uncanny sympathy for childhood and its clinging to whatever feelings keep it afloat. She is able to summon time and time again not just the right word but an inevitability of right words that create the trust we feel when we are in the sights of a genuine artist. She is able to find the images that insist on how much is at stake in any given moment. The confining actualities that a child observes with bated breath and that may send that child into squalls of tears or laughter are always in the forefront.

The trust one feels in Doty's art is far from pat, however. Doty prizes emotional honesty and is quick to catch the wry wrinkle in the clean fabric of what-should-be. Harvesting epiphanies is not her style.

She uses rhythm and form and (sometimes) rhyme to show how an experience—wanting to ride a mechanical horse outside a grocery store or touching a foxglove—surprises in its own right yet remains true to the stubborn clutter of human notions. Thus, a poem will dart along deftly to a powerful yet quiet denouement.

At its best, poetry manages the feat of being unerring and fallible at the same time, of communicating a simultaneous sense of the rich shakiness of the present moment and the hard weight of the past. Over and over, Catherine Doty succeeds in poems that are engaging, shrewd, and brimming with actual feeling. When I write "actual" I mean neither emotionally tethered nor shouting but willing to endure and celebrate the real emotional skeins and stains that constitute real lives. She has the knack and she knows how to use it.

—Baron Wormser
Hallowell, Maine

momentum

Catherine Doty

1

Yes

It's about the blood
banging in the body,
and the brain
lolling in its bed
like a happy baby.
At your touch, the nerve,
that volatile spook tree,
vibrates. The lungs
take up their work
with a giddy vigor.
Tremors in the joints
and tympani,
dust storms
in the canister of sugar.
The coil of ribs
heats up, begins
to glow. Come
here.

The Hungry Child

The child sleeps, her arm over the side of the bed,
trawling, the hand cupped, knuckles knocking wood.
Into her dreams swings the man from the TV show.
In his checkered coat, his polka-dot bowtie,
he scoops her from the cold and salty sheets,
flies her to his hideout, where she sees
a table just her size, and two red chairs
so small that when he sits with her his knees
bob before his smiling, wide-eyed face.
He serves her tiny, buttered red potatoes,
midget hotdogs that come from a little can.
There's rain, the sound of rain, the scratch of orange records
on the Mickey Mouse Victrola. "Tomorrow we'll eat the fishes
in the tin. We'll have a can of beer, and a bowl of white frosting."
This last sweet launches a sleep within her sleep,
deeper than dog sleep, a thick rug, a furry sleeve.
Morning comes, the cold walk to school, bells, prayers and milk.
The child opens books, waves her arm in the classroom air.
Then a walk home, and homework, and supper, and TV,
and sleep, that well of fulfillment, that deep warm pail of ocean
squirming with stars.

Wild West City

Before the cowboys blaze in to do their show,
loudspeakers blast from the sign over Kitty's Saloon
a warning for tenderfoots to skeedaddle away
if they happen to be in front of the blacksmith shop
because that is exactly the spot where they park
the horses. Soon seven monumental mustangs
face her. Their legs are velvety, veiny, their nose
holes drip. They are so big around she could live
inside one. She thinks of the plastic Indians home
in the toy box, scattered away from their ponies,
their legs a yawning O of disappointment.
Nearby the six-guns flash, but the horses are calm.
She memorizes their lashes, their mitteny ears.

On Monday the whole first grade Crayolas a farm.
Walt on her left draws chickens the size of tractors.
Raymond scribbles the grass, which is lousy with tulips.
The crayon she clasps gives her back her banging heart.
She draws the lathe-turned legs of the tethered horses.
She knows better than to draw their manes and tails
curly in that unicorn-sissy style. She recalls the way
the eyes and the twitching nostrils swell out
from the shoe box of the skull. The lips as soft as ashes,
and under the belly, with the tulip crayon she draws,
thick and strawberry pink, an anaconda, a curving,
knot-tipped bat. All day other sisters drop in
to see Sister Noel, to see the pigs on their hind legs
waving hello, to study the purple barn, the giant chickens,
the sun and the moon in one sky.

"For May Is the Month of Our Mother"

for Rosemary McLaughlin and Laurie Würm

When jump ropes smacked the softening tar
we took turns taking Mary home. She was white
with a blue screw-off bottom, supplicant hands,
and a rosary rattled inside as she swung in our book bags.
After supper is good for some, Sister Michael said,
*or before bed. If you pray the rosary, Communism
will fall.* When my turn alphabetically came for Mary,
I rattled her the two blocks up the hill,
but Catholic in our family was for kids, and Communism
was a word, not a stick or stone. My mother was tired,
my father was going to hell, I wasn't up to fifty Hail Mary's
alone, but I couldn't just dump Mary there on my cluttered dresser
like a glowing, white, wimpled bottle of shampoo
while I climbed the catalpa tree or played pies with the others,
so I set her down on our suitcase-shaped Victrola,
and put on Mom's Perry Como "Ave Maria".
Mary stood on her snake with her begging arms out, glowing.
The sky in the window grew orange, the breeze carried lilacs.
Next, I played Nelson Eddy, "Ave Maria". Her one-inch face

held too much sadness to bear. To cheer her up,
I played "Rum and Coca-Cola", the Andrews Sisters, and our souls
were so open from all that *ave maria* that we threw ourselves
into the rhythm, and jumped on the bed, and I beat Mary
like a maraca in my palm, her burden of black beads clacking
thick and loud, until one slap too many cracked her right in half,
and her beads flung themselves to the floor, where they lay
like intestines. I learned then to use something right
or leave it alone. No, I didn't. I learned *twelve-inch Virgin,*
polystyrene, luminous ivory, black beads in screw-off bottom
ran $4.95, or twenty weeks of allowance.
I learned too that Mary was real to crack like that,
and I saved a splinter of her shattered gown,
and I know she is patron saint of the spring-cracked mind,
and mother of all who aspire to glow in the dark.

Nun

The thought of your naked ears
woke us nightly, whining.
You, stuck in a huge black shoe,
crucifix slapping before your crotch.

For the slap of your long steel ruler
we soaped our palms.
They swelled like dough;
pencils flipped from our grasps.

Your fists! Bigger than Father's!
And your bras on the clothesline:
cups as big as our heads.

Breasts!

she yells, slapping the flat black front
of her habit, *everyone has them, they're what
you strike when you're sorry.* We are all
sorry. It's storming and blackboard-dark,
sky shot with chalk streaks, so Crazy Theresie
flies down from her own eighth grade
to act out The Stations. This she does
each time the good Lord obliges with thunder:
gives the fourth-graders a one-woman
Passion Play. *Jesus falls again!*
Like Howard Cosell, she captures
each thrust and dodge of the uphill
trudge, Veronica with her veil
swooping in like a bat boy. Hail ricochets
off the windows and right through recess
Theresie rips on, though our nickels
are on our desks and our eyes
are pleading. Soon Chuckie Reemer
turns gray and falls out of his desk,
adding his own dull thud
to the beat of the rain. Better yet,
Peter Palmer jumps up and grabs
two pencils, makes like he's nailing Chuck's
wrists to the dusty floor. Oh, it is good,
we are beating our breasts
like crazy. Passion shoots through us—
Theresie and Peter screaming,
the snap of his collar bone
and the crack of the thunder, the lightning-lit
eyes of the penny-bought
mission babies.

The Baby Book

First, the pages on human reproduction:
line-drawn ovaries poised like
prestidigitating hands.
She stares at them, wonders does
she have them inside her now,
or will they come when she's twelve?
Then plaster vignettes, like the Stations
of the Cross, cross-sections
of the uterus and its burden,
the opening cave and the baby's head
checking the weather. She grabs the pages
in slabs as thick as sheet cake, flips past
the lists of names and their origins,
sections on bathing and formulas,
the grave geometrics of diapers,
and stops at the best, last chapter of the book:
Things to Make with Children. Acorn brooches,
string dolls, yarn casserole pads, a boat
being carved from a soap cake.
In grainy black and white the soap slivers
curl from the knife like the wake of a wave.
Her own knife is too dull or her soap lacks wax:
chunks chip and scatter through the green morning light
of the kitchen. A boat is a craft, and a boat
is called a vessel. Where in this mess is the part
that you point at the sun? She feels her small life
bob on earth's glittering surface.

Eggs

We wanted to neck, like they did, we'd heard, at parties,
on couches with people watching us work our jaws.
We wanted to slug from a bottle, eyes rolled back,
but we needed a party skill so we'd get asked.
The library book said *a great trick for any party*,
so Evelyn and me, in her mother's kitchen, sucked eggs,
hard-boiled eggs, through the neck of a glass milk bottle.
A twist of newspaper, on fire, you put in first,
then set your clean, peeled egg on the bottle's neck
and the fire gets hungry for air and shivers it in
with a rubbery *BUP* of relief and a puff of black breath.
We told Evelyn's mom we were practicing social graces,
but she charged us a nickel a pop, called it playing with food,
and as each gray egg, flecked with shell, smudged
with carbon thumbprints, grunted like a spelunker
and shot its guts, she got madder, shaking her head
like a cat with canker. When egg number eight
slipped its hips and blew its brains,
she hollered she knew why we never got asked to parties,
and clean up this mess, and the cat box, too, goddamn it.
Evelyn wiped her hands on her yellow shorts,
smudging Davey Crockett's face with soot. We rolled up our mess
in the Friday *Morning Call* and went out to wander Chadwick Street
at noon, swinging our butts, and all our eggs in two baskets,
shivering with our potential to fuck with fire.

Mania

for Phyllis Ulivella

I loved the Beatles, too, but kept it hidden,
could not believe those photos of howling girls
shivering at Shea Stadium at dawn, the strings
of spit that laced their gaping mouths, and what
escaped me most: those pouring tears.
At school the confiscated Beatle pins
and magazines and dolls and trade cards grew
into a pile I dreamed of, and, at home, my sister
filled each minute with their music, a carnival
brightness beneath which I wondered, still,
what was it those girls thought likely to occur?
Was John or Paul or George (who was my favorite)
to pluck one lucky girl from that larval mass and—
then what, exactly? Meanwhile, back at school,
the boys were sent outside to clap erasers, while we
girls in our own private clouds of dust got a lecture:
The Sin of Lust, and this by a nun so white-faced,
sweated-up, and stuttery I was convinced the other
deadly sins had only random takers, like homely Ringo,
and took my place at dawn on the black macadam,
a light rain falling, and all of us wild-eyed and shaking,
awash in our mothers' perfumes, and screaming,
screaming, begging for John, the smart one,
or Paul, the cute one, eyes trained on the one lit gate
with the welcome banner, while the Boys slip in
behind in a battered truck, shot muffler blaring
a warning we drown in our weeping.

Sunburn

Again and again
we grease our supple skins,
spread ourselves on the earth
that wants us back,
think we'll go slow
but evening finds us sick,
feverish and weak
in our baths of tepid tea.

Here's where I try to say
this might be like love:
turning ourselves 'til
no single cell is spared,
thinking, as pinwheels rage
beneath our lids,
I'll stop before anyone knows
what a fool I've been,
I'll rise from this
just as soon as I'm beautiful.

This Might Work

The worst, and my favorite
page, was the Health page:
that freshly showered
or ocean-dipped girl,
her handsome fingers
ribboned with trickling water,
wrapped around the waist
of a sweating glass.

Where was that girl
when I needed a loyal sidekick?
My best friend used two numbers
instead of a name
and wasted whole days
in Honors English
insisting, for example,
that *Grandpa's nuts*
was the possessive-declarative case.

What hope was there for us?
We ate cake, and loved the idea of pie.
We stood
beneath our own windows,
tossing up stones and catching them
in our teeth.

Mrs. Vooren's Calendar

Each time her son would crap
she'd write it down: EBM
for Ellsworth, Bowel Movement,
though she was a cockney
and called it *moving your barrels,*
which put me in mind
of dragging the trash cans in
a moment before Zito's bread truck
sent them spinning. Once, at our house,
Mrs. Vooren and my mom talking,
Ellsworth tore out of our bathroom,
yelped out *yes!,* and Mrs. V.
popped up like a prairie dog,
grabbed a black crayon, and scrawled
EBM on my mom's new calendar,
three tarry letters as thick as clusters
of flies, under smiling Miss Rheingold
ablaze in snowy skiwear. Our mother
preferred not to know what came out
of us, and when once I managed
to go in the Voorens' bathroom,
where a fifty-pound net bag of onions
slumped next to the tub, I told her
I'd gone, and she just snapped,
You flushed, yes, m'duck? and shoved
me outside to read comic books with Ellsworth,
that cosseted turnip, that prig, that mama's boy,
that temple of virtue, that little sack of shit.

Outside the Mainway Market

Every day, our mother says,
kids die on those goddamned things,
and she nods at the lone yellow horse
with the red vinyl bridle
and four black, shining hooves
like police hat brims.
Not only do we stop our five-part
begging, we walk wide around the beast,
though Mary brushes the coin box
with her sleeve.

Rigid in flight, the great horse's legs
flange out toward us. Not one of us argues.
We hold onto our mother's coat, cross
several streets, touch the dog we always touch
when we walk home, fingering
his freckled snout. Then we scream
and run in the yard while supper cooks,
and the sky shudders pale for some seconds
before it darkens, as if in that lavender moment,
three blocks away, a child drops
the reins and gasps as his shoes fly off,
and plumes of smoke rise
from the crown of his hand-knit hat.

A Woman Who Liked Babies

A woman who liked babies
went in and out, in and out,
like a bright toad's throat
her stomach went in and out.

Sometimes babies came of this,
and sometimes she went home alone,
but not for long.
The other babies all at home
were so happy to see her back
alone or with another one.

How sad this woman
was alone! When her baby stayed
because it died.
When she went home to the babies there
she acted happy, but she cried.

Her babies at home didn't know.
Or they did.
She always carried something in—
a bakery box or a baby, you see.
Once there were cupcakes for Halloween
because the baby's cord was wrong
and once yellow cake with jelly between
when a baby was born with its heart too big.

The ones at home were so glad
she was back,
and the littlest acted a baby again.
They tried to feed her bits of their cakes

but she was busy with messes to clean
and babies to mess with in between.

Now the ones who were babies
are grown and they've fed
on cake after cake.
There's been little bloodshed.

Lassie Comes Home

to the old Terhune place in Wayne.
He catches the kung fu flick
at Movie City. The nunchakus fly,
the blond guy is always master.
Fetch this, mutters Lassie,
hiking his leg.

Three Texas wieners at Libby's,
a pitcher of birch beer—
heartburn and heartworm take root
in his glorious ruff. *Good dog*,
belches Lassie, licking his chops.

Soon he'll be back to saving
and saving that kid, that boy in bangs
who's old enough to shave, yet falls
every week through black ice
or slides into silos brimming
with breathless grain.

But for forty-eight more hours
he's his own best friend,
free of the furious lights that dry
his coat, the cameras that whine
in a pitch he alone can hear.

For two precious days
let all eight-year-olds swallow skate keys,
drop small girls like dumplings

to simmer in Barbour's Pond.
No whistle can make Lassie run
like the girl he's not,

he's off to kill a few pigeons
near City Hall, where the meat-rich reek
of the curbs smacks of genuine danger.
He's weekend-wild as a boy in a prep-school
blazer, thickened with joy
and bred for beauty and good.

52 Canal Street

The house, of course, is gone,
the sled path's steepness
flat as the hopscotch slate path
gone now too, birchwood,
violet bank and pear tree gone,
forked ash where we oiled
my sister's wedged knee free
felled, with the three black cherries
in a row, gone their sweet black berries
small as peas, clots of bright sap,
black bark to peel like sunburn,
and back-hoed into the ruin,
animal graves, cat-killed rabbits
and parts of rabbits, the cats, too,
knot-headed toms wrapped in pastel scarves,
phosphorescent decay and bright small bones,
shoe box and match box and brown paper
grocery bag, boxer dog under where once
stood a stand of grape, all the rich good
that we children gave stroke, bite and kiss,
and the only dollar we had once, rolled up
and fed to the hole in the bathroom wall.

II

Home for a While

I know my mother is the mother of sorrows.
This is my litany:
I live alone.
I work two jobs.
I will come home.

She knows where each green point
breaks the frozen ground,
how to force the poor tomatoes
with slabs of glass.

Thunder rolls in the yard.
I want to run to the cherry tree,
slap its bark,
come back before it rains.

Oh manacled fist of the phone!
I am dancing crazy.
I let something slip:
say *our house* or *our cat*
and she hears.

Mama—this smoky kitchen! this veil of tears!
No use.
Her very hands are sad.

Through the window:
old women in housedresses,
big as houses. Cherry bark.
Thunder. And rain.

Gratitude

One day we were big
and our mother got a job
and she knitted herself two vests
to wear to work
a green one with a turtle on the pocket
a good one, she said, to wear
while filing cases
and one of a blue, diaphanous
sparkly fuzz that made her
look like kin to the water cooler.
She loved to work, loved the office
across from the courthouse
the pigeons and the poor
around Eva's Kitchen
where occasionally the hungry
got surplus Popsicles
and pitched the sticks
in the bushes in front of
the courthouse, bones
of a food that couldn't
nourish, that couldn't
be saved or sold. Our mother
thought of our poorness
then, of when we were little
of letting us eat the rolls
from the go-go bar dumpster
the guava jelly and quail eggs
and cans of soup

that showed up on our steps
one Thanksgiving weekend
and gratitude came over her
like an ecstasy, gratitude
came off her like steam
for her gorgeous job
her restaurant lunches
thank you thank you thank you.
She all but curtsied when a pill cup
of macaroni appeared unbidden
next to her pastrami.
She brought home pastries
window-boxed like orchid corsages
clipped recipes, warmed up pot pies
bought cream, fruit, nuts
an electric knife
thank you thank you thank you.
At her metal desk in the corner
she filed her frauds
and on payday rushed to the bus
as we ran from our jobs
to meet in her yellow kitchen
to tip back our graying heads
to be healed with fatness.

Horror Today

The brother prone to nosebleeds shuffles in,
the chest of his pajamas brown and stiff.
The mother coos his name and runs a bath.
She dabs at his cakey nostrils, his rusty chin.
Soon she sets out the scrapbook, tape and such.
One face appears to be melting, one whiskered snout
tips up in a howl-at-the-moon, a rubbery gout
of brain marks a drooling eye socket ringed in sludge.
October's *Horror Today* has all great things
except, largely, bodies, even horrible bodies aren't scary.
You really want scary, try adding a head, *that's* scary.
Tom cuts out an early Wolfman, the kettle sings.
He eats the inside of, she the outside of, pie.
They both like the monsters best that still look like men.
She stutters the scissors through fur, slime, and mutable skin.
He cuts around Mudman, the Feeder, the Human Fly.
Days, days, days and days will pass like this—*Monster, Eerie, Creepy,
Phantasm, Mad.* Shooting from their pale eyes beams
of staggering power, mother and son codify and keep the dreams
of those churned, at night, into savages, those merely sleepy.

French Coke

When her children visit they gather in the kitchen.
She moves among them in an ecstasy of giving,
opening bottles of beer for them, frying eggs.
Remember, her daughter will say, *that Christmas Eve,*
when Mommy got schnockered on cream drinks
and cried because Maurice Chevalier was dead?
Remember Sunday mornings, her horrible records,
the Easter chocolate gone oniony and wet
in that swamp of a fridge? Remember her thinking
the Coke in that crummy French restaurant
came from France? The litany of ridicule continues,
without malice. They kiss her when they leave.

She and I are not the sleepers we were.
Sometimes we talk all night, dozing and drifting.
We roll into each other as softly, as accommodatingly
as the cats in their flowered chair. She is like an armful
of lilacs, fragrant, fragile, so soft I can number her bones.

The children go home and leave us, old clowns,
to our rounds. In five different houses they're reinventing sex.
In their brightest rooms babies waken and savage the air.

My Father's Hats

The Yankee cap he wears today
keeps from his face the gnawing sun.
Under its stiff and once-blue brim,
a crosier of smoke and last night's blood.

A second hat, atop the first,
brim backwards, lends him rakish grace.
He rolls like Sisyphus the rock
of his slow tongue, and, hatted twice,

makes slow through the chalked
and toy-strewn walk, gold leaves above,
concrete below, nodding to where it seems
he's been, as well as to where he hopes to go.

Landscape with Pony Track

You'd think the rich stink of pony
would rule the senses, but violets, sunflowers,
hollyhocks draw the eyes, which dart
from the shaggy Shetland's horrible privates,
a-drop and a-swing like the backstage works
at Saint Ag's, to a bank of tiger lilies, those carroty stars.

Two girls, the sides of their sneakers
worn away, wearing tattoos of water paint
rubbed on with spit, check it out:
this heaven of leather, fried onions, and music,
five houses from where, with no eyes for flowers
or horseflesh, their father's face reaches
the texture and twitch of skinned hare.

Outboard

A drinking buddy gave our dad an outboard motor.
Dad kept it, up to its orange chin in bilge,
in an oil drum, up in the yard, and, after a few,
he'd go out and start it up, yelling, *Get back,*
you kids!—but we were already back, and ready to bolt
if the green plastic men we'd thrown in up and busted the thing.
But no tiny, acid-stripped skeletons churned to the surface;
the army remained at rest with the worms and the pear cores.
All that spring, when he felt good, he'd go watch his motor,
his nostrils straining to catch each oily fume,
a Chesterfield dropping ash down the front of his work shirt.
Once Shaky Louie, his pal, braved the terrible sunlight
to join him in motor watching, and, chatty by nature,
told us Dad had said soon that our freezer'd be so full of trout
there wouldn't be room left for even one skinny Popsicle.
By August we'd scrawled SS DAD on the slimy oil drum,
but he never noticed, just stood in the din, smoking, staring.
He never did lug that motor out of the oil drum—
he let winter do in the only toy he had, though it spat
muddy rainbows and roared like a locomotive,
and gave off the piercing and molten stink of hope.

Living Room

Remember the Halloween night
I was sick with migraine
left alone with you
while the others went out
and we took your nap together
after the beer
you on the couch and me
on my back on top of you
I could smell the painted flames
on my devil costume
the devil's starchy mouth hole
damp with beer
I could see the car lights
stripe the living room ceiling
hear Halloween banging
at the door
hear your breathing
turn to sleep breathing
as I lay full-length
on that bony, crabby daddy
that man who never touched
who hardly talked
I was happier than I had ever been
I was petting a sleeping lion
I thought of turning five
the next day
I thought of the cake
the paints and paper
I'd asked for

a picture I'd make you
of two red devils sleeping
of bowls of candy
safe and untouched in the dark

Roses

Whenever I try to dissolve
that man in hatred
I picture him coming home
early from work in late May,
two quart containers of ale
bubbling foam in his fists.
Our mother says
Look Brad old Piney's protecting his roses
and we hold up our shirts
so he sees on our stomachs the gouges,
the dark glyphs of blood,
the lesson we learned from old Piney
who dragged from his brush pile
the harshest dead rose canes
and lashed them to our fence.
Then our father sets down his ale
and kicks open the door
and runs up the yard like a man
who never runs
and tears at the barricade of inch-thick canes
'til his hands become bloody dog jaws
and his yellow nylon shirt
is a butcher's shirt
and he heaves the canes
so they land on Piney's porch
and he stomps past us into the kitchen
and gets his ale
and escapes from us into his bedroom
where it's cooler

and stinks less of bleach and frying
and crying kids.
And then every room of the house
bursts with yellow roses
with cream and pink and white and russet roses
to carry to school in glass milk bottles
for the Virgin
and to bury our faces in
dizzy from that sweetness

Broom

Three windows
and the dead
black tips
of fig and rose
at each white sill
and dancing
still past stove
and pot
pale chicken
in its watery thaw
I stroke your neck,
your wooden back—
you bring me luck—
taut, taut, slack, slack.

The grit that flies
from your coarse skirt
is what we live:
salt, crumbs of crust,
gray and blond
and chestnut hair.

The boys look up
and lift their feet
then drop them
like four heavy books.
What wisdom do boys hold
for us, who read now

only flame and floor?
You lead, I follow,
dust to dusk,
to where you'll hang
behind the door
to rest there, dark,
who'd rather fly,
but, wooden, sees
what roots are for.

Care

Unconscious, insensate, two-dimensional, punctured:
this is the man I dream of as a child. I lean from my rocker
to gentle the dull hair back, lift from a flowered bowl
a dripping cloth, wring it and press it to the ribs and the wound
between them. Someone else has plucked the bullet out, arranged
the blankets and pillows. At the door, where they lean and yawn,
those useless boots. My specialty is the moist hand over the heart,
music of falling water. If he lives, a few spoonfuls of scrambled egg.
He's any of the Three Stooges, or Circus Boy, or Mr. Greenjeans,
that big straw hat on the bedpost. Every day at three or four or five,
he climbs an elephant or jigs a puppet, dresses to keep my interest,
leaps to please me. He is a flicker of light, is all potential. Tonight,
when I close my eyes, he takes a bullet.

Dosage

Meatloaf tastes more homemade in any diner
than in the dining room of any home—much like
the boxy vignettes in the furniture stores,
so welcoming nobody argues the rubber croissant.
And the bedspread on the fake bed smooth
as marzipan—not like your own bed, that moldy
rack of contagion, containing, in four years' time,
your twin in dead skin cells: one wanders and tries
to be tender, one sleeps triple shift.

And sometimes you try medication to keep things buoyant,
colloidal in that chowder pot of a brain. *Happy pills*
somebody said, as if, plumped like a pillow,
the soul on such stuff glows and spins like a disco ball:
mood lighting, mood lightning, go ahead, step on my foot.

Well, it's not like that: your life is still lipped and sticky,
the needle trees ringing the property ring loud as ever.
But behind you the thoughts drop like breadcrumbs:
benign, digestible. Sidewalk may offer its mica: twinkle, twinkle.
And sometimes the crabs, who scuttle in bitter sludge,
cast off their spiny shells and come pliant as hands.

GI Joe, Buried in Seaside Heights, 1972

Because this is how long it takes,
he is purely refreshed.
The pale ochre cap of his crew cut
glints like ore; lamp lit,
he squeezes out, a strong-jawed parsnip.

Inside his vinyl skin:
more beige-colored vinyl.
He's skin-deep to the core.
In a ceremony of kisses
he was buried.

Before him, the same rental cottage
as years before, another shade
of whatever's this gray
at midnight. Billboard with a car
on it, elbow of road,
coarse sandy spit of divider.

The water tower looms,
an idling space ship.
Joe's on his back, shivered sand
and yellow pebbles.

From the cottage: plumbing noises,
clink of dishes. It's like that under
the earth, but slower, slower. Not like
how people think: that it all stays put.

The Head as Head
of the Household

At four the plates of the skull
are not quite bone—
they shift like a funhouse floor
as underneath
our children go cataloging
their first mild griefs,
burying turtles in handkerchiefs,
and learning to lie
as we do when
some thing in our own shifty heads
tells us our catalog is long
and sorrowful, tells us to choose
from a dozen the sweetest mudpie.

Stoop

The sun rising—
tire swing glowing
like a donut sign
on a lonely highway.
This is the forest
god-awful: cars
in their morning sweat
like overworked horses,
dew on what grass there is,
and bed sheets doing
for drapes in the bachelor's
bay window. Once Willy said
If you eat M&M's
you'll die. He was two,
he was desperate, I didn't
touch his candy,
so I live, big enough
to steal anybody's chocolate
and, more important,
by hours the first one awake.

The black cat next door is starting his motorcycle—
no he's not, he's trying to mount
the neighbor's tabby
who's thinking about
what she's going to kill
for breakfast, maybe a garter snake
or a baby wren.
On Jersey Street, a steep

one block away, the crackheads
and winos sleep, leaving the storefronts
blank and bright as bird song.
There's coffee in this cup,
and in pavement cracks
peppermint plants its feet,
advancing, shining. Then Henry
appears in his Mickey Mouse
underpants, and says, *Mom, write
once on a time, we both woke up.*

Whole

A butter knife looks like a sword
in a three-year-old's fist.
He stands at the table,
bread held across his chest,
buttering everything between shoulder
and shoulder, so that when he tosses
the slice down on the table
a butterless bread-shaped spot
remains on his blue shirt.
His fingers shine, his eyes
shine, his hair is yellow.
I think of the person-shaped
hole a person makes
when he blasts through the wall
of a house in the morning cartoons.
I ask, What are you doing?
He's buttering again. *I'm doing this,*
he says, *so my heart won't break.*

Is it working? But he knows
to be quiet now, knows there's a red
vinyl change purse, a sugared cookie,
paper-of-love, the pink foil box
from chocolate, all of them sweet and cheap
and fragile and common. And somewhere
there's his heart, which, so far, is sound:
he hasn't heard it crack, like the tiny toy men

he leaves scattered on the floor.
He hasn't caught me sneaking it into the garbage
with other things snapped or damp or missing
pieces. The sword flashes, dull as cardboard,
the butter flies. I stay where I am,
and the fist-sized heart is whole.

III

Why I Don't Drive a New Car

for Stephanie Back

On the spring nights we drove them home
our first cars were beautiful:
sprung seats padded with greasy pillows,
chrome corroded, dings as endearing as freckles
and, when we leaned on the horns,
nasal bleats, foggy duck calls, or low and solemn farts.
We named our first cars:
Perdita, Joe Pickle, The Mermaid.
We had so many places we wanted to go.

Some mornings, when we weren't home
but waking up,
the sight of our cars from a second-story window
was all that we had to lash us to the earth.
When one of our cars was broken
our friends roamed the terrible cities
to find us in front of our houses, waving and frantic,
and took us into their cars,
safe between their laundry and their lovers.

And what was as pretty as young, unbreakable bodies
tumbling from old Volkswagens at Sandy Hook?
And, if a parent died, what rich consolation
we felt at the sight of a dozen or so of us
spilling like clowns from a Day-Glo painted Valiant.
No, I don't need to be nagged to buckle my belt

in a voice as cold and fake as a Burger King milkshake.

Here's to a car that a pal can puke Southern Comfort in!
Here's to a car with a creamed corn can for a muffler!
Here's to the discontinued and disenfranchised,
longing for those parts no longer available.
I'll drive my rusting bones in a clamoring wreck,
a car like our first cars,
the cars that we loved
when we thought that we knew where it was
we wanted to go.

Shame

She knows what it's called
when you borrow
and don't pay back,
but she goes
when her mother sends her,
then sits out her shame
in a wrecked Chevy
ringed with puddles
near the tracks,
a box full of springs and sticks
and knobs and wires
so rusted she cannot tell
what its color was,
and she sets on what's left
of the dashboard
the tepid milk
in a baby bottle, sour
around the neck,
a dollar bill rolled up
like a cigarette,
and a cigarette,
and watches the orange sun
slide like something wet
off a grayish plate
into the blackberry thicket
along the fence.
At twelve she's too old for milk,
too scared to start with dollars,
cigarettes are like baseball:

she doesn't get it.
When she wakes
the tracks are white veins,
the banked gravel black.
Each oily puddle
grabs all of the ripening moon
and gives it back.

Figs

for Bob Carnevale and Denise DeLeo

The first fig I ever tasted came over the fence,
the Polish man next door plopped it in my palm
and pointed to the tree about to be wrapped,
that tree that in its winter burlap coat looked so
like a tied-up tornado you'd piss your snowsuit.
It was too good, too good, the texture was ticklish and crazy.
Renée, who lived where fig trees went naked all winter,
said that figs piled up and rotted under her tree,
told me that often those pools of tarry gut
were fluorescent with bees.

Fig trees pop out their fruit without fanfare,
without one flower, the figs themselves being flowers,
tender bellies, pocketbooks full of wet blossoms. A fig
is not picked, it's redeemed: figs drop from their branches
as if leaping to rescue below, so soft, so soft,
they rarely survive their fall. And now you two stand
in your driveway in your socks, loading my car with baskets
and bags of figs, and with you and your fig-shaped cat
growing small in my mirror, I eat, humming into that richness.
I croon to these figs a song of fig-sweet friendship,
and of crossing the tar of New Jersey,
mouth brimming with flowers.

Foxgloves

So homely
in July
wiry spires
of rust
but pet them
or brush them
with your passing
hand
and peppery clouds
of seeds
lay claim
to the earth

biennial
like certain kinds
of grief
a tuft of puckered
pale and leathery
leaves
next May is
a swaying tower
of open mouths
pink or pale yellow
freckled, ruffled

waving—
in each tender cup
the furry back end
of a bee
watch now
as one backs out
like a drunken boy
bobbles in the glare
of afternoon
and bumpily rushes
to find that sweetness
again
not in the place
he was
but in one
very like it

Outside Cat

After she presents her kill to me
I touch her for the first time,
betrayed as she is by her heat.
I sit with her over the mouse
she's mauled to stillness,
stroke from her throat the grudging,
rusty purr. She teases
with her needle teeth my fingers,
crazy for any touch. I am a sorry version
of a mate. The gift of a mouse is meat
and fur and scurry—products
sane people covet every day.

3 A.M.

At 33 I lived inside a car,
two offices, a bar, a restaurant:
I wanted any life that wasn't mine.
And with a dry chianti, flowers, toys,
would visit, visit, visit, my settled friends,
read to their kids and wrestle with their dogs,
go home too late, too full, too shallow, empty
and watch from my porch the ancient two
next door, screened in, at cards, no way
that they could sleep, so busy, iced tea
to carry to their lips. Between them,
on a tray, those dry cookies children hate,
a salami cut in coins, and a tall, pale
cheese with holes in it—Jarlsberg? Swiss?

Today

I love the women in the deli:
two with handsome hands and doctored yellow hair.
They wrap my corned beef sandwich with crisp affection,
they give me extra mustard, extra napkins.
They remind me of the two blond girls in the country,
climbing their flatbed of sweet corn mid-July,
giving me thirteen ears instead of twelve,
giving me change: their sore little green-brown hands.
All steamed up, I carry my leaky lunch
to a rock in the park where I can't sit still to eat.
I could raise a child, I could save a person's life
or write a song. Each thought is thick as a fish
with connecting thoughts, every word needs
to be shouted and choreographed. I haven't slept
in three nights; soon I'll tip over, forget
that I'm swollen with God on days like these,
forget yellow food, bright day, flowered shelf paper,
dogs, radio, and the smells of cement and rain.

Curriculum Vitae

And every mistake you learn from:
the paregoric nips at the Paul Simon concert,
forgetting that six-year-old boys are babies,
really, not short men with loose
front teeth, track in fourth grade and the name
you earned: Reverse. All the attempts,
like the fish tanks of your childhood,
begun in eager greed and soon to fail:
twenty-five gallons of well-lit bouillabaisse.
And the fudge you rushed, running off the side
of the table, a curtain of shit. Remember red
eye shadow, lasagna in Iowa, planting a sprig
of mint, saying *call any time*, sneaking
the cat on the plane, really sending that letter?
You wrote your resumé in this cool new way,
you left the stew pot on with the flame real low,
you wore white pants, no bra, your sister's tiara . . .
you used the word *you* when you knew the word
was *I*—you wrapped up the whole shebang
with *I need this job.*

Naming the Appliances

Blend, stir, crush and pulverize—
the single constant is the roar. We call it *roar*,
then turn our eyes to the drop-hinge door
on the dish device that seats in stadium rows
and scours the china: *box of hammering streams*.
And, also, there's the slashing storm
contained in that acrylic sphere, which *nuts to soup*
we call—that thing which bids zucchini disappear
then reappear as nacreous chips or pour like magma
from its lip. Witness now the *smash the trash*:
enough! This premise falls apart—it pales, it shreds,
it rinses clean. Whole be our innocence, bright its worm,
bless certain beasts and some machines and grant us,
God who holds the purse, dominion over what we curse.

On the Anniversary of the Opening of the Erie Canal

a wedding poem for Amy and Tom

The earth opened for them.
The water obeyed them also—
this would ease their lives,
that's why they did it,
joined together what had been born
asunder. What they did
made the earth better.
It was good.
So they shot off cannons,
they sang on the banks
and ate chicken.

Faith like they had
brings us here. Faith
that licks smooth the earth-sad
broken stone, that gives it shine,
that buoys us through the tributaries
of grief: faith like water,
rising and reflecting.

What banks can contain such rushing
wealth? What lonely towns will be
named by you?
What we celebrate today improves
the world. We bring with us our Canons
and our Nikons. We cheer

the overland journey
that brought you here.
We want for you, Amy,
we want for you, Tom,
what you have: faith in the water's
ecstatic, rushing gift,
love of the obstinate earth,
its fireworks and picnics.

In Search of the Concrete

for Renée Ashley

Start at the foot of the stairs,
where a bag of 5-20-10 spills
its nourishing dust, and, if among
the sacks of grit and spunk
you see in four-inch letters, REDI MIX,
stop there. If not, creep further in,
and try behind the furnace, the garden box,
the blood meal and its maggots
and the rags, where once the cat
set seven squirming kits, their winking paws
the size of fingertips, and root your hand
between the rakes and hoes. No luck?
What luck was ever yours? You cannot name
or claim what's in your heart. The words
despair and *love* are less than dirt,
less than the urine-colored light
that seeps through a crack you would fill
if you could find that sack of dust
to which you can't return.

White Light

A woman, dying, waits for white light,
for opalescent wings in the sonorous air,
or maybe two enormous, glowing hands,
cupped to enfold—no, that's an insurance ad,
and this is dying, more serious of course,
and so, ashamed, she sobers up and waits
for the time she's put in so far
to pass before her. She could have been better,
she knows, not one perfect meal, not clever
with love, and way too many men.
In a chrome-and-white blast, she pictures
every kitchen, including the card table,
hot plate setup in Wayne, then the peach
and cocoa and pink of all those bedrooms,
nothing, she thinks, but a tedious inventory.
The movie slows and she sees, chronologically,
the grave of every cat she's ever owned,
beginning with Katie, who, wandering off
in sickness, collapsed, she now knows,
in VanHouten's cubbyhole. Poor manly Emily,
tucked in beneath the pear tree, ochre-
striped Fred and his glossy brother, Minnie,
wrapped in silk scarves in a rented yard
in Montclair. The love she wants to give them
is hurting her. She hears a moan, and the cup
appears again, summons her back to the lip
of the life she would leave now.

Hansel and Gretel

Why do they always go into the forest?

At its rim they pause to collect
the black-green curls of the last sweet chard,
and with one swift look at the parents
who cannot feed them, enter, obedient,
the prickling black cathedral, the icy pines.
Of course, when they're starving, their house
of cake appears—the freckled, gingery shoulder,
redundant icing—they nibble until
they are captured and brought inside, faces
glazed with shame and snot and sugar.

Do you suppose that the mother who sewed red flowers
on the little velvet bodice, the green suspenders,
then counted the cupfuls of flour, the mouthfuls
of sausage, and muttered, *Oh, damn them,
send them to the witch*? Witches must eat, too, and some
witches must eat children. I bet that gingerbread
house was a thing of beauty.

Then there's the part of the tale where they trick
their hostess, where Hansel says, *that's no chicken bone,
that's my finger*, where they flip the witch
into her fire and pilfer her treasure. Then burdened
with precious jewels, they rush to their parents,
dropping an emerald here, an opal there.
The world, you see, is then brought round to right:
oily joy coats the cottage walls like soot.
The children are home, and the thick muck floor of the forest,
becrumbed with jewels, outsparkles the pocky ink
of that other sky.

Momentum

Your friends won't try to talk you out of the barrel,
or your brag to go first, which has nothing to do with bravery.
And you're so hungry to earn their love you forget
to claim first your, perhaps, last look at this mountain—
crab apples hanging sour in the sun, abandoned Buick,
a favorite place to play, dismantled and weathered
and delicate as a voting booth. Instead you dive straight away
and headfirst into darkness, the steel drum that dusts you,
like a chicken part, with rust. Looking out, there's nothing
to see of your friends but their calves, which are scabby,
and below them the filthy sneakers, shifting, shifting,
every foot aching to kick you off this cliff.
Their faces, you know, are blank with anticipation,
the look you see when they watch TV eating popcorn.
They're already talking about you as if you're gone,
as if you boarded a bus and roared out of earshot,
when one foot flashes forward and launches you.

You know as you feel that first solid slam you are lost.
The barrel changes shape with each crash to earth,
as you will later, assuming and losing lives, but this
is so true now: ankles flayed to the bone, cracked ribs
and crushed mint, the brittle, pissy sumac. Right now
the pin oaks are popping in their sockets, the hillside
wears your shoes, clouds pleat and buck. You know, of course,
that no one's going second, and friends who tell this story
will use the word *idiot*, rolling their hands in the air,
but you know you know what your life is for now and rise up,
and just about scalp yourself on that tree limb above you,
another thing you couldn't possibly know was coming,
another which, like your first breath, was not your idea.